SMALL GROUPS IN THE CHURCH

A SPURGEON'S BOOKLET

Small Groups in the Church

KEITH ROBERTS

Series Editor
Paul Beasley-Murray

KINGSWAY PUBLICATIONS
EASTBOURNE

Cover artwork by Ron Bryant-Funnell
based on an original design by John Herbert

British Library Cataloguing in Publication Data

Roberts, Keith
    Small groups in the church.
    I. Title   II. Series
    260

ISBN 0–86065–848–1

Co-published by the British Church Growth Association,
St Mark's Chambers, Kennington Park Road, London SE11 4PW

The BCGA gratefully acknowledges the help of the Drummond Trust.

Printed in Great Britain for
KINGSWAY PUBLICATIONS LTD
1 St Anne's Road, Eastbourne, E Sussex BN21 3UN by
Richard Clay Ltd, Bungay, Suffolk
Typeset by Watermark, Hampermill Cottage, Watford

Preface

Founded in 1856 by the Victorian 'Prince of Preachers', Charles Haddon Spurgeon, Spurgeon's College is an evangelical Baptist theological college located in south London, which over the years has trained many hundreds of men and women for Christian leadership both in the UK and overseas. Spurgeon's has always had a strong emphasis on vocational as well as academic training. It is only natural therefore that, with Kingsway Publications, Spurgeon's, under its Principal Paul Beasley-Murray, has teamed up to produce this present series of booklets, which aim to cover a wide variety of pastoral issues.

Before becoming Principal of Spurgeon's in 1986, Paul Beasley-Murray served with the Baptist Missionary Society in Zaïre (1970–72) and for thirteen years was Pastor of the Baptist Church in Altrincham, Cheshire (1973–1986).

Keith Roberts is Pastor of Mitcham Lane Baptist Church, Streatham. Previously he served as Pastor of Laurier Heights Baptist Church, Edmonton, Alberta (1981–1982), and as Pastor of Catford Hill Baptist Church (1976–1981).

Contents

Introduction

Garfield was 'discipling' Nermal. Today's subject was about climbing trees:

'Follow me, Nermal. This is how we climb trees,' said Garfield.

Upon reaching a precarious branch at the top of the tree the following brief conversation was overheard:

Nermal: 'Now what do we do, Garfield?'

Garfield: 'What a silly question, Nermal. We sit here until the fire brigade comes!'

Why do we do some of the things that we do in the local church? Sometimes there are good reasons and clear purposes which give real meaning to the activities we invest our time in together... yet, sadly, other activities can seem as meaningless as climbing trees seemed to Nermal.

Given the pressures and the pace of life, it is really important that the time we spend in church activities is well spent. This has been increasingly recognised: in recent years there seems to have been a move towards better stewardship of time which is linked to activities that are of value for the life and mission of the local church. 'Church growth' thinkers have been in the forefront of this approach.

One of the outcomes in many churches has been the rise of the small group movement. The rise of home groups has been most significant. However, some seem to have got the impression that all you need is small groups and you'll have a growing and purposeful church... 'Take ten people, a comfortable room, tea and coffee, copies of *Songs of Fellowship*, Bibles and hey presto... meaningful small group life!'

There is a danger – either of churches simply jumping on to a small group bandwagon without giving sufficient thought as to why, or of churches who have already jumped on to the bandwagon giving up on small groups because they have lost whatever meaning they did have.

It is as easy for small groups to become lacking in purpose as for any other local church activity. The sad thing is that many have become convinced of small groups as the answer to church problems, to the extent that small group life is not subjected to the same scrutiny as other areas of the church's life.

It is my belief that as local churches we still have much to learn about the significance that the small group can have in the nurture, development, and equipping of Christians, and in the life and mission of the church. This belief grows out of having seen and experienced a

10

wide range of small groups in the past six years, both within and outside of the local church context. These six years have included time in North America seeing how small groups operate in a number of churches, including the Vineyard Fellowship in California; two years in a Clinical Theology Association Human Relationships Group; working through the Fuller Seminary syllabus on small groups; experimentation with a wide range of small groups in our own local church; involvement in various training opportunities with small group leaders in other churches; and also work with small groups at Spurgeon's College.

Let us get back to Nermal. He really had two questions. The first was, 'Why climb trees anyway?' and the second was, 'Having climbed them, what do you do next?' These two questions can be addressed to small groups in the church. First, 'Why have small groups?' Secondly, 'Once you start them, what do you do with them?' The answers to these questions are crucial.

Sometimes the answer to the first question seems to be little more than, 'It's what others are doing, and besides, the experts say it works.'

The reply to the second question seems to be an equally unconvincing, 'Just let them carry on.' (Or, in Garfield's approach, 'Just stay there until the Lord comes.')

If small groups are to be meaningful for the participants, and are also to make a positive contribution to the life and mission of the church, then we need to find more purposeful answers to those two questions. We need a clear initial vision of the role of small groups, and then a developing vision of their full range of possibilities.

John Stott, in *Issues Facing Christians Today*, defines vision in the following way, 'It is an act of seeing, an imaginative perception of things, combining insight and foresight... compounded by a deep sense of dissatisfaction with what is and a clear grasp of what could be.'[1] If small group ministry is to develop and flourish, then each of these ingredients needs to be present.

First there needs to be an *imaginative* approach to the possibilities of small groups. We can so easily get stuck in small group ministry. There are two very practical ways of stimulating an imaginative approach to small groups. One is to look around at what's happening in small groups in other contexts. You can do this either by reading and researching, or by visiting other places where small group ministry is being carried out helpfully. Doing this will encourage creative approaches to small groups in your own setting. It will help you to ask the 'Why' type questions which are so important. A second approach is to set members of your existing small groups, and the rest of your congregation, to 'brainstorm' on the ideas for small groups which they would find meaningful. Usually they scratch where they are itching in a way that preprogrammed packages don't.

Secondly there needs to be *insight*. This is the quality which enables a person to understand the true nature of something: in this case the true nature of small groups with all their dynamics, advantages, dangers, and also the true nature of the church's ministry. I believe, with regard to this insight into small groups, that time spent as a member of a small group outside of the local church context could be an invaluable insight for many Christian leaders.

Thirdly there needs to be *foresight*. This is the ability to make provision for the future. We need to see how small groups will relate to the future life and development of the church. This aspect of vision will guarantee an ongoing process of leadership development, and also a willingness to be constantly reviewing the present small group programme in the light of future needs and opportunities so that necessary pruning can take place. Small groups lend themselves to this type of review as they are potentially the most flexible structure in the local church.

Fourthly there needs to be an element of *dissatisfaction* with things as they are. Some love change for change's sake, and others hang onto the status quo at all costs. As far as the development of small groups is concerned, there needs to be a dissatisfaction with any approach to small group ministry which either disregards the basic principles of small group dynamics and opportunities, or which trivialises the time spent together in activities and relationships. Nothing is more likely to kill a group than spending important time on trivial matters.

Finally there needs to be a *clear grasp of what could be*. This requires hard work on the part of whoever supervises small group ministry in the church. Time given to reflection, reading, exploration, conversation and prayer, will be time well spent in which vision can become clarified.

So the vision needs to be developed. This is true particularly with regard to the ways in which we use the Bible in small groups. This concern will filter through the whole booklet. In the first section of the book we will look at some ways in which vision can be developed. In the second section we'll look at some of the 'Hows' of small groups.

PART ONE

Why small groups?

1

Created in God's Image
For Relationship

Theologians have debated for centuries what it means
for people to be created 'in the image of God'. One truth
they all seem to agree on is that it is to do with the facts
that we are created as personal beings, and created for
relationships. In his book *Created in God's Image*, A.A.
Hoekema, in commenting on Genesis 1:26–27, says:

> What is being said is that the human person is not an iso-
> lated being who is complete in himself or herself, but that
> he or she is a being who needs the fellowship of others, who
> is not complete apart from others.[1]

This need of relationship is underlined in Genesis
2:18 when pre-fallen man is, by implication, said to be in

need of more than simply relationship with God. When we are not experiencing honest and open relationship with others we are living against our humanity. Again, Hoekema on Genesis 2:

> Not only is man incomplete without woman and woman incomplete without man; man is also incomplete without other men, and woman is incomplete without other women. Men and women cannot attain to true humanity in isolation; they need the fellowship and stimulation of others. We are social beings... It is only through contacts with others that we come to know who we are and what our strengths and weaknesses are. It is only in fellowship with others that we grow and mature. It is only in partnership with others that we can fully develop our potentialities.[2]

So the caption of the poster on my study wall, printed over two chimpanzees hugging each other, sums up the profound biblical truth that 'We need each other!'

The small group is a place in which these kinds of personal relationships, which we have to experience if we are to mature as human beings and as Christians, can take place. A book was published a few years ago with the title *Crowded Pews, Lonely People*. The title indicates that true relationships cannot really be experienced in the larger gatherings of the church. The person who lets everything out to their unknown neighbour at 'Come Together' or some other sort of celebration event, is not experiencing what Genesis is talking about. Such sharing best occurs in the context of a small group in which people have a degree of commitment and accountability to each other.

Genesis is saying that these relationships are basic to human life. Sadly many are finding these relationships outside of the Christian community in a plethora of small group experiences which are based on secular principles and are often 'selfist' in nature. It is time that the church got its act together and explored how to develop small group ministry in a way that promotes such necessary relationships.

The small group experience can be one of knowing and of being known; of loving and of being loved; of laughing but also of crying together; of being affirmed but also of being challenged and confronted; of sharing the most significant experiences of your life but also of playing games together; of worshipping God together with intimacy, but also of getting our hands dirty together serving him in a variety of ways in mission to his world.

The small group can be all of these things, yet sadly at times it is none of them. Some people can remain in their 'aloneness' even within a small group setting. This can be for a variety of reasons. We shall look at three of the most common, which, if addressed, could bring a renewal of life to many groups, as they would facilitate the necessary relationships that Genesis speaks of.

The *first* is to do with the simple and yet complex pressures of normal daily life. How many times has each one of us gone along to a small group with churned up feelings within us about the day's events? We have found it hard to join in and share in the evening because the day's events have got hold of us and are on our mind. Let me give you an example.

I was recently leading a series of training evenings for small group leaders in another church. As people were arriving for the second session, which was on a Friday evening, I sensed that a number of people were exhibiting all the signs on their arrival of wanting to be somewhere else. They looked quite tired. So we changed the agenda and spent the first ten minutes or so in twos telling one another about the day – what had been significant for us and how it had left us feeling as we'd come out that evening.

Words like 'frazzled', 'really tired', 'frustrated' and 'rushed' all surfaced. But as each one told their story to another, a sense of release was experienced. No longer was anyone alone with their day, and, as a result, their involvement in the group changed. Each one said that they now felt more able to engage in the evening. They were no longer just house group leaders training for a role, but they were people who had shared themselves with each other.

A regular time to share early on in any small group gathering can help us break through from aloneness to relationship where growth can take place. We are coming to meet with each other, so let us meet as we really are on each occasion. This encounter can be the material which the Holy Spirit takes and uses to make the group a growing experience for each of us.

The *second* is to do with the guilt or sense of failure that we sometimes manage to carry around with us as believers. We seem to have this capacity to imagine that we are the only one in the church, or in our small group, who is not perfect yet. This is often compounded because at times we display a lack of integrity in our sharing. We are quick to share victories but not defeats. We are ready to speak of encouragements, but not discouragements. There is nothing worse for contributing to aloneness in the small group experience.

John Wesley showed his pastoral wisdom in the rules established for the early Methodist small groups. One purpose of the gathering being:

> To speak each of us in order, freely and plainly, the true state of our souls with the faults we have committed in

thought, word, and deed, and the temptations we have felt since our last meeting.

Questions to be asked each week were:

What known sins have you committed since our last meeting?
What temptations have you met with?
How were you delivered?
· What have you said, thought, or done, of which you are in doubt whether it be sin or not?

Such a direct approach might seem a little too rigorous for the small groups in your church, but certainly we need to explore methods of enabling members of small groups to break out of the winter of their aloneness with their sin or sense of failure, into the springtime of confession, restoration and burden bearing which the New Testament speaks of.

Listen to the wisdom of Dietrich Bonhoeffer in his *Life Together*:

> He who is alone with his sin is utterly alone. It may be that Christians, notwithstanding corporate worship, common prayer and all their fellowship in service, may still be left to their loneliness. The final breakthrough to fellowship does not occur, because, though they have fellowship with one another as devout people and as believers, they do not have fellowship as the undevout, as sinners... in confession the breakthrough to community takes place.[3]

So a regular opportunity to confess those areas of failure and struggle in our lives within an environment of love, acceptance and forgiveness, rather than one of suspicion, censure and rejection, will enable us to move from aloneness to fellowship.

The *third* factor which can contribute to a sense of aloneness, even within a small group, is the fact that within our increasingly transient society, all that is known of us is what stands before the eyes of those we meet with. They know little of our history and the factors that have conspired together to make us the people that we are today, with the dreams and fears that we have.

Why is it that after twenty years of living in London, the first football result I always look for is not Arsenal's or Spurs', but Cardiff City's? The answer certainly doesn't have anything to do with the quality of the football team! It is simply that having been taken by my grandfather to Ninian Park regularly when I was a youngster, there is part of me that is for ever Cardiff City! They are part of my history.

My roots matter to me and so do yours to you. On numerous occasions in small groups I have encouraged people, who were otherwise quiet and seemingly on the outside of the group, to tell us their story. Invariably this exercise has enriched the human contact between members of the group and helped a sense of belonging for the individual. The Serendipity approach to small group Bible study refers to this as 'the story telling' stage of group development.

> This phase is so basic that it is often forgotten until group members wake up months later and wonder why they feel like strangers to one another. Your past; where you've come from – your roots, heritage, significant people, places and events that contributed to the person you are today is very significant.[4]

So we are created for relationships and can really only grow as human beings and Christians through fellowship with other people. Small groups can help to facilitate those relationships, particularly if they become places in which we can share who we really are, how we really are, where we've come from, and what are our dreams for tomorrow.

2

Created in God's Image
For Rulership

In the early chapters of Genesis we discover a God who
makes decisions and who exercises sovereignty. Then
in verse 26 of chapter 1, we find this God deciding to
create people in his own image with authority, dele-
gated by himself, to rule over the earth. It would seem
clear that part of being in the image of God is that we
are given areas of personal rulership, decision-making
power and responsibility. Dr Hoekema comments
helpfully in *Created in God's Image*:

> Most interpreters... have believed, and rightly so, that
> man's having been given dominion over the earth is an
> essential aspect of the image of God. As God is revealed in
> Genesis 1 as ruling over the whole creation, so man is
> pictured here as God's viceregent who rules over nature

as God's representative. Having dominion over the earth is essential to man's existence.[1]

When I was younger there was a popular song that reflected this rulership in a sentimental sort of way. The first line said, 'If I ruled the world every day would be the first day of spring, every day there'd be a new song to sing.'

The fact is that neither the author of this booklet nor its readers are ever likely to be in a position to try out our theories of world dominion! However, each of us is in a position to exercise a degree of responsibility, decision-making, rulership and even sovereignty to an extent, over our own personal worlds.

A significant development in recent years has been the rise of the 'self help group'. Whether it be Gingerbread, Alcoholics Anonymous, Parent Link, or a group of students joining together as a study group, the point of each of these groups is that people in similar situations, each with needs and goals in mind, come together to acknowledge their situation, their desire to grow and develop and their need of support and accountability if this is to occur.

The key to many of these groups is that they provide supportive contexts in which people can actually learn to handle the circumstances of their lives, the challenges and opportunities before them; and in many cases significant growth occurs.

The individuals involved can experience the sense of significance and fulfilment involved that comes from growth, development and personal responsibility, within the context of good relationships. In the secular context, part of the image of God is being expressed in such small group relationships.

This concept of a small group in which believers can grow by assuming personal responsibility in the context of supportive and accountable relationships, is an essential contribution to the sanctification and growth of people within the church, especially when such groups are allowed to address the real situations that face people: to explore what it means to live Christianly.

For example, in our own area of London, multi-faith RE has become an issue for some parents and teachers. This is an area in which Christians often hold strong views, which, to me, seem to suggest a misunderstanding between the role of the church as an evangelising agency, as compared with the role of the school as an educational institution. Often a lot of heat and little light is generated.

Some Christian teachers have found it difficult to do anything but comply with the militant Christian point of view... Nevertheless, some have continued to do so with unresolved questions and inner tensions on the one hand; or, on the other hand, they have reacted with frustration and anger to the lack of understanding, on the part of some, to the actual classroom dynamics and context.

In response, we have established a small group context in which teachers from our own and other local churches, as well as local teachers of no faith at all, can look at some of the issues and make their responses in a non-threatening context. This helps their growth as Christians in that it enables them to assume personal responsibility for their own decisions and professional lives. Even though you or I might not agree with each decision that each teacher makes in this context, I would contend that to the extent that it enables them to assume personal responsibility, it contributes to this aspect of the renewal of the image of God within them.

Sadly, again in this area, small groups sometimes fail in their task. This is because it is possible for the approach to small groups, especially as they relate to decision-making and responsibility in people's lives, actually to contradict this particular aspect of being created in the image of God.

The *first* reason is that sometimes an agenda can be imposed upon a group which doesn't reflect the real life agendas or situations which its members are facing. This can be a danger in churches where groups are centrally organised or controlled, and are tied in to a particular study programme. But if a key issue in small groups is to enable its members to live more Christianly in a secular context, then it is essential that reasonable time is given to dealing with the real life issues of its members.

This is why I believe that a reasonable percentage of the small group life of the church could helpfully be given over to peer groups of one sort or another, whether age related, interest related, or life situation related. Within a few weeks of writing this, over 60,000 Christians will gather at three different centres throughout the UK for Spring Harvest. One of its pulls is a whole range of common interest seminar groups. Why can't such groups be a more regular part of the small group life of the church, or group of churches? When we are running small groups that address the issues concerning a person's life, then biblical truth is far more likely to be translated into action, decision-making and responsible living, in a way that reflects this particular aspect of the image of God within us.

The *second* reason is because, even in the small group context, some Christians find it easier to assume responsibility for the decisions and lives of other Christians. They find this easier, rather than going through the painful experience of working through, with those who are struggling, the implications of growth in personal responsibility and decision making.

Of course we are to be supportive of one another, the Scriptures make this clear. But we are to encourage one another, so that each of us can more fully live out the life of the Spirit in our own unique way. We must make our own decisions (certainly in consultation with others) which will include mistaken ones as well as correct ones.

In their most helpful book *On Being Family*, Anderson and Guernsey speak of the major tasks of parenting. The third task is particularly significant to the small group experience. It refers to the task of separation and individuation:

> Healthy parents raise their children not to need them. They work themselves out of a job... what is at stake is the child's sense of mastery of its own world apart from the mother, and the freedom to fail if necessary and to know that its failures will not end in catastrophic loss or disaster... What the child needs is the reassurance of the care giver that her presence and support can be depended upon and that as a child ventures out into the world the care giver will be a steady source of support and encouragement. The message must be 'You can't go wrong if you grow up. It's okay not to need me. I'm with you even if I don't do things for you.'[2]

This is exactly the sort of autonomy, responsibility, and decision-making power that we need to encourage one another to exercise. Sadly there are some Christians who find it easier to let others assume responsibility for them, while at the same time there are always those within the church who are happy to control the lives of others and be needed by them.

Too often than should be the case, the pressure is towards group conformity which actually works against this particular aspect of the image of God within us.

A *third* factor is a slightly different version of the last one. Here the individual can abdicate responsibility to God himself.

One of the major differences I experienced in the first small group that I was part of outside the local church context, was that once people had shared what was going on in their lives and what they were planning on doing in response, we didn't all pray for one another. It seemed strange at first, although eventually it became quite liberating. It is not that I don't believe in prayer for one another. It is simply that within that group it became apparent that each of us was personally responsible for responding to the insights offered, that we were not handing over responsibility for the outcome to the Lord.

I believe that God is at work in each believer both to will and to carry out his good purpose. But having said that it also seems that some small groups are in danger of handing over to God those areas of personal decision making and responsibility that he has freely entrusted to us. When prayer in a small group results in corresponding action on the part of members, fine.... but when prayer results in an inactive waiting for 'my flesh life to melt away' or for the Lord to make it so clear that there's no decision to make anyway, then I believe something is wrong.

We are then in grave danger of a small group life which is working against the image of God which the

Lord is attempting to recreate in our lives.

So small groups have huge potential in the area of growth into maturity on the part of Christians... providing within those small groups we recognise the individuality of members in their personal situations, and also facilitate a responsible approach to life and decision making which is chosen by the individual while being supported by the group.

3

The Growth of the Church
Only Where Relationships are Strong

We've looked at how small groups can relate to two aspects of our personal nature as people created in God's image. Now we'll move on to see the need for small groups to be a place in which relationships can flourish, community can be built, and mission can be released, for the sake of the health of the Christian church.

The New Testament makes it clear that the church is not primarily an organisation, but an organism: a living community of people who through their relationship with Christ have been drawn into relationship with one another. The quality of these relationships affects the life of the church. This belief is summed up in the following quotations:

> The true nature of the church is relationship... loving personal relationship to God and to each other as Christians and as human beings. If healthy, loving, personal relationships are lacking, there is nothing to knit the church together around the Head. In effect, there is no church.[1]

> To be or not to be a community is not an option for the church. By nature the church is a community and experiences communion. But the question before the people of God is: What kind of community will we be?[2]

> Although there is no one correct form that the church must take, it does need to be a community.[3]

The church is built up and relationships are strengthened when there is a context in which lives can be shared, and ministry of various appropriate kinds given and received. Others have written so extensively in recent years on this subject that there is little need to repeat what they have said.

However, if we are to get into the sort of sharing of life together that builds relationships, strengthens the church in its living, and motivates its members for mission, then certain logs which contribute to a log-jam in relationships in small groups need to be removed. Clearly one of the greatest barriers to relationship is our own personal sinfulness. We shall not look at that here as many others have done so already. We shall restrict ourselves to looking at certain 'structural or group-centred logs'.

Barriers to relationships

The first is *blandness*. My dictionary defines 'bland' as

'mild in flavour, insipid, dull, soothing in manner'.

That's exactly how some small groups in the church context seem to be. There can be an abject lack of getting to grips with the real issues which are occurring in people's lives and the accompanying impact on their attitudes, feelings and behaviour.

Such groups can be pleasant for a while, are usually far above the water line, and totally safe in a sterile sort of way. Few risks are taken, little growth occurs in the participants, easy answers are offered, and challenge or the conflict which often accompanies it is avoided at all costs. This is because such encounters are always seen as negative, destructive, and somehow less than Christian. Often the leaders of such groups imagine that they are protecting the members of their groups, whereas, in reality, they are usually only giving evidence of their own inability to handle strong dynamics.

If a small group does not exhibit a willingness to question and challenge as well as accepting and affirming its own members, then it will contribute little to the purposes of growth for which it was established. The problem is that we can become intimidated by some of the dynamics around the challenging growth points in a group experience. The danger is to back away and fail to use the situation as it is presented.

An example will illustrate what I mean. Anne was a member of another church. For a while I was involved in running some small groups with this congregation. She was a gentle person who always tended to hang back in group situations rather than offer the undoubted insights which she had. She had been in various groups within that church, but had always been passive. No one had actually addressed this in any of the groups she had been in and I felt that little growth had taken place.

Eventually she joined a group whose specific purpose

was to pursue growth into new ways of relating. For the first couple of weeks she said nothing apart from one or two pleasantries. Her shyness was apparent to all. Then, on the third week, the leader of the group asked her how she was feeling about saying nothing. Immediately you could feel tension within the group. People knew this had been a no go area, and there was threat and disturbance around. However, with gentle encouragement on the part of the leader, she began to say how it all made her feel. There were words and there were tears... There were also long pauses during which some members of the group clearly felt uneasy and would have preferred to get on to something less threatening. An opportunity had been given to her to look at an area of her life which, up until then, had been avoided. Over the months that followed, a number of changes took place in her life, slowly and gradually. Through all of these changes she was supported by the group, and increasingly she made contributions to the group. She has now begun to retrain for a new career, has started to drive again for the first time in years, and helps in a significant area of ministry in her local church. The stereotype she had lived with for many years has begun to be broken and she is now exploring some of the dimensions of her life in Christ.

One important fact about this group, which we shall look at again, is that each of the members had 'contracted in' to explore these very life-restricting issues. It was not a Bible study group, and yet we actually obeyed many of the scriptural injunctions concerning how to build one another up. So often what we need to make group life meaningful is less Bible study per se and more Bible application.

The second is *boredom*. Some small groups simply die of boredom. The problem is often compounded because we've been led to believe that small groups as such are the answer. Therefore there is a reluctance to bury the group! It seems wise that small groups be operated on the basis that they have a limited life expectancy. If, for example, a group is meeting weekly, then it has to reckon on some sort of 'death' or 'renegotiation' within at least a twelve month period.

The major factor in boredom in a group is a lack of purpose which is allowed to go on without being addressed. This can occur for a variety of reasons. Possibly the group didn't decide on their reason for being in the first place. Or maybe some of the group members didn't really understand the purpose and so came with a range of differing expectations, which, when not met, resulted in boredom.

Some groups suffer from a lack of purpose because someone in the group hijacks the group for their own purposes. It could be they have a pet subject that finds its way into every Bible study. Or more likely the group becomes the place of support for one member's needs. It is fine for this to happen providing the group sees what is happening, acknowledges what is happening, and agrees to it. But often nothing is said openly, and a number of people become increasingly frustrated.

Other groups suffer from boredom because the necessary skills, support or input are not available to the group to address its purposes realistically. Again, sadly in some churches this fails to be recognised and someone eventually ends up as the scapegoat.

Small groups really do need adequate supervision that is not intrusive, but facilitative.

One final factor in boredom in a group is that no review procedure is built into the group from the outset. We have found it helpful in some of our small groups to offer each member a review sheet after two or three months in order to get feedback from each member to discover how they are experiencing the group, and their suggestions for its development or otherwise.

Another way of facilitating this sort of feedback is to have one or more coordinators of small group ministry who are available to sit in with the groups on occasions, to help them to look at themselves in a way which encourages honest reflection.

With regard to the danger of boredom setting in as a result of lack of purpose, the importance of a contract is central. Dr Roberta Hestenes of Fuller Seminary makes this point very clearly:

> A Christian small group can be defined as a deliberate face to face gathering of three to twelve people who meet regularly and share the common purpose of exploring together some aspect of the Christian faith and discipleship.
>
> Within this general definition there are many different kinds of groups with differing specific purposes. Healthy small groups need a clear sense of purpose shared among the members. A group promise is a shared understanding of the purpose of the group, with an agreement on the general means that will be used to achieve that purpose. Groups experience difficulty when there is no clear sense of direction or commitment by all the members. The process of discussing and defining the group promise is called 'contracting'.[4]

Let me share an example of contracting from our own small groups.

First there was precontracting which occurred before the group began. We offered people a choice of various small group experiences. One, entitled Exploring Prayer, was being led by myself. The precontracting was carried out by giving those interested enough information about the general direction of the group and the methods we would probably use so that they could make an initial response.

Then there was the confirming of the contract. This took place at the first group evening. For us this involved a sharing together of how we might approach the subject, what people had in mind as they decided for that particular group, and certain very practical arrangements about how long we would meet for. A couple of very helpful suggestions were made and agreed on. A couple of members of the group who did shift work said they would have to miss part of the course and we were able to change the times to help them up to a point.

Finally there was the review stage. This was an evening at the end of the group when we evaluated the group together and looked to see if there was anything that could be improved for next time.

So we had clear boundaries and feedback was being asked for. This is a healthy way to maintain and renew a sense of purpose. It will usually safeguard a group from boredom setting in.

The third is *bureaucracy*. Again I've consulted my dictionary. It is defined as 'government by the officials of a central administration; such officials often being regarded as inflexible or unimaginative'.

This is where I'm in danger of being accused of being either subversive at worst, or totally impractical at best!

Most experts in small group ministries seem to agree that one of the major advantages of small groups is their flexibility. Howard Snyder in *New Wineskins* speaks on this advantage:

Because the group is small, it can easily change its procedures or functions to meet changing situations or to accomplish different objectives. Because of its informality it has little need of rigid patterns of operation. It is free to be flexible as to the place, time, frequency, and length of its meetings. It can easily disband when it has fulfilled its purpose without upsetting the institutional seismograph.[5]

Yet sadly some churches are quite inflexible as far as their small groups are concerned. It seems as if small groups are sometimes log-jammed by the issue of 'control' or 'ownership'.

This problem relates either to the purpose for which you operate small groups, or to the view that a local church leadership has about their task.

If small groups are seen purely as the forum in which people can work out the material preached by the minister on a Sunday, then obviously there is only a limited flexibility to the way the groups function. If the groups are seen as a general pastoral care structure for the congregation, then more flexibility is possible. But if small groups are seen as a 'way of life' for the congregation, it becomes possible for greater initiatives to be taken by members with regard to the range and usage of small groups.

However, each of these approaches is affected by the way that the minister, elders, deacons or whoever, see their leadership function. Usually the 'control' of an area of a local church's ministry rests with the leaders of the church. This causes a significant 'bureaucratic process' to come into play. When this happens with regard to small groups, there can be a significant restriction in the flexibility of approach, and also in the extent to which ownership, responsibility and authority for the small group rests with the group itself. This can hinder life and initiative from the grass roots.

Larry Richards in his book *Biblical Principles of Church Leadership* poses these three questions in relation to the ministries of the local church:

The Issue of Ownership of a Group — Who is Responsible for a Ministry Area?

The Issue of Consensus — Who Makes Decisions About Ministry Areas?

The Issue of Preserving Freedom — What Role Belongs to the Church Leaders in Relation to a Ministry Area?

He answers his first question by saying that a ministry is the responsibility of the Lord Jesus as Head of the Church and of those that he has called to that particular ministry (or group). Therefore only those involved in a particular group can be responsible for it.

The second question is answered by saying that those who are responsible for a group make the decisions concerning it. This is done on a consensus basis of decision-making.

The answer to the third question is that the leaders in the church are not there to make decisions for others in the church. They are to affirm Christ as Head. 'What leaders can do is to give insight, suggestions, support and sometimes advice to help the responsible parties make good decisions.'[6]

This approach would give increased freedom and flexibility to those involved in actually leading the small groups. If alongside this the church leaders could appoint a coordinator (or coordinators) of small group ministry who was a person with insight into the working of small groups, then such a person could be an invaluable resource to those doing the job. In addition from time to time the church leaders might well believe that a certain type of small group was appropriate for the church. For example, in our own church last year we believed it to be wise to offer our people a range of Special Interest Groups. These were offered. Some were not responded to at all, so they did not function. Some were very positively responded to and became the 'possession' of the leader involved in the life of that group. The group members also exercised a degree of ownership as outlined in the 'contracting' process mentioned earlier. The role of the church leaders from that point was to be available as a resource for those leading the groups as and when required.

4

Church Infrastructure
Where Do Small Groups Fit In?

In this chapter we will look specifically at some of the
ways in which small groups can fit into the total structure of local church life. Peter Wagner has popularised
the idea of church structure summed up in the formula,
Celebration + Congregation + Cell = Church.[1] Each of
these groups has functions, activities, and behaviour
which is appropriate to the groups. We sometimes fail to
recognise the appropriate purpose and activity of each
size of group. To do this is to steal from each grouping
its own distinctive possibilities.

The 'Cell' or small group is the primary group. This is
where life changes can occur. It comprises ideally three
to twelve people and its focus is on personal involvement
in the lives of one another as members. Its distinctive

ethos can be summed up in words such as 'intimate face-to-face contact, vulnerability and personal encounter'. This type of group is a place in which the members can share feelings, needs, hopes and generally address what is burdening them. This is the environment in which personal development and growth can take place in the lives of the participants.

Not to use small groups for such purposes is to rob them of their opportunities. If group members remain in the objective mode without sharing the implications of what they are learning together for their own lives then little will be achieved.

One author has described small groups as the place 'where ugly frogs can be kissed and transformed into princes and princesses'. That implies closeness and vulnerability. So let us look at certain 'small group appropriate' activities, and also at how they could work out practically in a local church.

First there is the group that could best be described as a Bible study group. If churches have small groups at all, the chances are that they begin with this type of group. Here, as with other areas of learning in the local church, there is a need to overcome the danger of being theoretical. The need for many of us is not to learn more about the Christian life, but to learn to do and to live what we already know in theory.

The small group can be the place in which people grapple with the implications of the biblical teaching they have received as members of the congregation. It is an opportunity for people to reflect on teaching, question themselves and each other, and decide what this means for them in their daily living. The truth to underline here is that we are not to be into mere discussion of biblical texts, but once having understood the text, the issue is applying it to life.

For example, within one group, after some teaching on financial giving and stewardship, the members decided to spend the next few weeks looking at the implications. Without any outside pressure or interference they decided to share with each other the details of their regular incomes, the differing circumstances of their lives which affected how they could use their incomes, their giving to the local church, their support of other ministries or charities, and finally how they could increase their giving as individuals.

As a result of this desire to apply the teaching, two really good things happened. First the members of the group did increase their giving, and opened up a bank account together which helped to finance certain 'ministry projects'. But perhaps equally importantly they came to a new understanding of one another as they talked for possibly the first time about areas of their lives which had been hidden. One couple had parents who had been missionaries and were reaching retirement with nowhere to live. They were contributing to their parents. One married lady with an unbelieving husband shared some of the restrictions placed on her by her situation. One member of the group, who was significantly lower paid than the rest, shared how that felt and how stretched she sometimes was. Significant growth occurred.

Secondly there is the 'kinship' type group which usually centres on the 'one another' ministries of the New Testament which we know contribute to the building of individual believers as well as to the church as a community. Again the key here is 'to do the stuff'.

There is a wide range of mutual ministry that comes under this banner in the New Testament, including: accepting one another, encouraging one another, admonishing one another, serving one another, praying for one another, bearing with one another, bearing one another's burdens, confession to one another and honouring one another. The danger is that we simply analyse these areas of ministry rather than actually do them.

There are a few helps to facilitating these ministries. The first is to train leaders of such groups to realise that their major contribution to the group is to be regularly modelling the behaviour needed within the group. This will mean both giving and receiving such ministries. Leaders need to be ready to share where there are personal discouragements so that others realise they too can be vulnerable and can receive acceptance and encouragement from the group. They also need to be sensitive to the needs of others in the group to receive these ministries. This will involve a lot of careful listening not only to people's words, but also to their behaviour, body language, and facial expressions. The second will be to guarantee that there is regular opportunity for people to share with one another how they are, what is happening for them, and what their needs are on any given occasion. The third is to make use of those group materials that can help release such ministry. The most helpful that we have come across include *Life Together* by Post Green Community, Serendipity Studies, and the guides to such ministries written by Gene Getz and published by Victor Books.

Thirdly there are those groups which to many people feel slightly more risky. These are groups which begin with the experience of the group members. Such groups explore who we are, why we respond in the ways that we do, how other people experience us and what we can learn from their feedback to us, and how we might grow and change. These groups are always very intentional in nature and in my experience of being a member of such a group, and also a facilitator of such groups, their impact can be very significant.

These groups will tend to use 'exercises' or 'games' to help each member to get in touch with themselves and how they feel and respond in different situations. Significant time will be given to allowing members to talk about themselves and their life experience, with the intention of enabling the members to come to a better understanding of themselves and what makes them tick.

To give an example of what I mean, I will refer to some groups that I and three others have been running at Spurgeon's College with two groups of students recently. The students were invited to join a group which would help them to explore some of the following areas of their lives:

Discovering and accepting previously unknown or unacceptable parts of themselves.

Learning how to express feelings, especially in terms of what bothers us about ourselves.

Exploring how others experience us in a group context.

Experiencing affirmation and security within a group, while at the same time experiencing the adventure of growth and risk taking.

The basic resources of such groups are the members themselves, and their own experience and willingness to reflect on that experience. Obviously there is also a need for people to facilitate these groups who have a degree of self-awareness and also training in leading such groups. Such training is readily available from a number of sources, and in many churches there will be those who in the course of their professional work development will have undergone such training.

Two models that will often be used are first 'Johari's Window' and secondly the 'Learning Cycle' model. These can be represented visually as follows:

(a) Johari's Window

Open Known to me Known to you	*Closed* Known to me Unknown to you
Denied Unknown to me Known to you	*Hidden* Unknown to me Unknown to you

Often in small group life we deal primarily with the 'Open' window. Those areas about ourselves known to both of us. Within this area of our lives we can offer support to one another. However, there are other windows which contain great opportunities for us to grow. The 'Closed' window has the power to isolate me from you. This could cover areas of fear, anxiety, dreams for the future, etc. The 'Denied' window concerns those areas of my life that I am either unaware of or which I successfully deny as being true. These areas are known to you, but are not normally mentioned. The fourth window is the 'Hidden' window which includes those areas unknown to me and to you.

In the context of a small group who have contracted together to explore growth, the 'Closed' window can become a resource through confession, while the 'Denied' window can become a resource through honest feedback to each other.

In a group I was involved in recently, there was a member who very clearly benefited from insight into the 'Closed' window. Regularly in group meetings he would speak about himself in such a way that would elicit quite a degree of sympathy from other members of the group. As the weeks went by he was more and more seen as a victim of circumstances. Eventually someone tentatively offered him some feedback which suggested this to him. While it was a necessarily painful journey for him, he began to see that one aspect of his lifestyle which was hindering his growth as a Christian, was that he tended not to assume responsibility in his life, but rather let life happen to him. This has become a significant growth point which probably could not have occurred without such a group experience.

The Learning Cycle model acknowledges first that we learn from both formal and informal learning experiences. Within the church we tend to concentrate on formal learning which usually takes place through such means as sermons, Bible studies, training courses, etc. However, much of the learning which affects our lives is informal, through experiences like talking with friends, family life and intuitive insight.

(b) The Learning Cycle
(Taken from *Making Adult Disciples* by Anton Baumohl, Scripture Union)

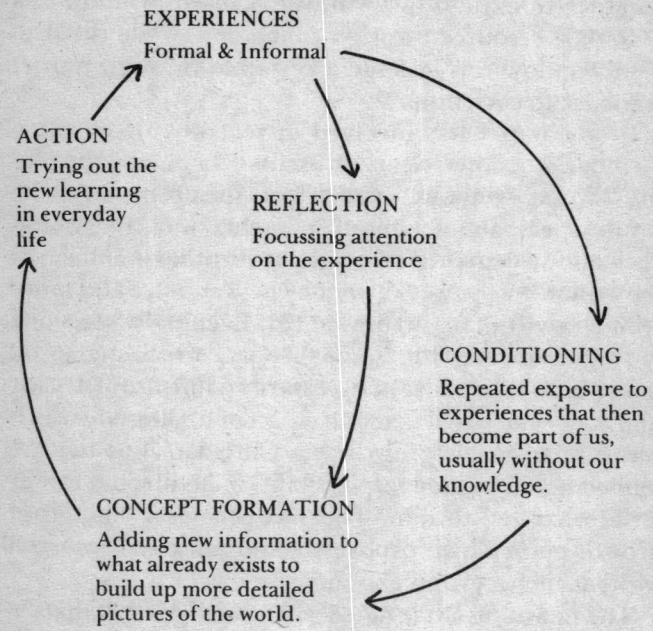

EXPERIENCES
Formal & Informal

ACTION
Trying out the
new learning
in everyday
life

REFLECTION
Focussing attention
on the experience

CONDITIONING
Repeated exposure to
experiences that then
become part of us,
usually without our
knowledge.

CONCEPT FORMATION
Adding new information to
what already exists to
build up more detailed
pictures of the world.

The model recognises secondly the need to be able to reflect on these learning experiences. For most of us as adults, we are so rushed that we need a context in which we can reflect. Otherwise we move to the conditioning stage. Some conditioning is good, but clearly some is unhelpful and not conducive to Christian growth. Hence the need to reflect and unpackage our experiences.

Once we have done this we move into the stage referred to as 'Concept Formation'. We have added the new information to our lives as a result of reflecting on our experiences and we are now in a position to make decisions which will affect our actions and experiences in the future.

The small group can be a very good context in which to carry out such reflection, questioning and growth. But it begins with people's experience rather than academic Bible study.

Fourthly there are small groups which can function as support groups to equip people who are going through similar life-related experiences. These are very much on a par with the self help groups mentioned in chapter 2. Again these are face to face encounters for those who are eager to be equipped in a particular area of their life.

I have referred already to a group that we run which is for those involved in RE in local schools. One of the very interesting facts in the way that group is developing is that, whereas at first the concern was only about syllabus issues, now the teachers, both Christian and unbelieving, seem to be sharing also some of the struggles, questions, and uncertainties that they experience. It is developing into a very real resource at a personal level.

In this area of support groups the sky is the limit, providing there is a willingness to be a little flexible, as obviously people do not want to be out at meetings every evening of the week. But how about groups for those in the caring professions with their distinctive pressures? Maybe a group for people who work in industry or commerce to share how they handle the pressures (or don't). A group for first time parents, or for those who are one parent families. These groups should contribute significantly to helping people to live Christianly in their out of church context in a way that other church activities might not do. They can also have meaningful evangelistic impact.

And, finally, there are 'mission task groups'. So often the local church as a body assumes responsibility for all the activities that could be summed up as mission. Then we attempt to find people to staff these ministries, often with considerable difficulty.

We've said that small groups are the context in which personal development and growth can occur. As followers of Jesus we believe that to be people who are developing and growing, we need to be people who are becoming servants of others. The personal growth we are speaking of is not to become preoccupied with the self!

Mission task groups allow small groups of people to meet one another and to serve together in an area that they feel drawn towards. Frank Tillapaugh outlines this philosophy to small group life and the mission of the church in his helpful book *Unleashing the Church*.

These small groups assume ownership of the group and then have to work through the implications of their chosen area of ministry. While church leaders are available for support and consultation, the members grow through the very fact of their personal responsibility for the group and its mission.

Within our own situation there are a number of these groups. One group serves our local community through a Parents and Toddlers and a Pre-School Playgroup, another through a weekly soup run and associated activities with some of the homeless community of Central London. Another group has recently been exploring some of the implications of urban mission, while another group makes banners for our church buildings. The possibilities are endless! But the ownership of, and responsibility for, the groups needs to belong to those involved in the groups, with support being available where necessary from the church leadership.

PART TWO

How small groups?

5

Developing a Strategy

In the first part of this booklet we explored some of the 'Why' issues. We saw that there are all sorts of ways in which small groups can be used in the local church. In this second part we shall look more at the 'How' issues. How to go about beginning or developing the small group approach in the local church.

While there are certain dynamics of small groups which will be common to all small group situations, there are also some significant differences which will be affected by the specific purpose(s) which you choose for your small groups.

The purpose you decide upon will affect various strategy issues such as:

How will the groups be started?

Will the groups have a basic or general function in the

church, such as providing a basic structure of pastoral care or working through of the public teaching material, or will they have a more specialised function? If the answer is a general function then the groups will probably be started from the top, whereas if the function is more specialist they are more likely to begin from grass roots.

Who leads the groups?

Which skills are needed? Different types of groups need different types of leaders. While all leaders of small groups need to be at ease in personal relationships, other skills will vary according to the purpose. A growth group will require certain skills that a mission task group will not require. If you can't sew it's probably not a good idea to lead a banner making group!

How often does the group meet?

A kinship group will probably meet weekly, while a support group for those in a particular profession might only meet on a monthly or bi-monthly basis.

How long does the group meet for?

A skills training group or study group related to a specific project will meet for anything from six to twelve sessions, whereas a kinship group would probably meet for a year. A training group might meet for an hour's duration each time, whereas a kinship group would probably take the best part of an evening.

How big is the group?

Obviously a small group is a small group so there will not be fifty people in it. But a mission task group can probably handle more in the group than a kinship group. Also if you are using groups for training, it is quite possible to offer input to twenty-five people for part of the session and then let them subdivide for training exercises into smaller groups.

Who can join the groups?

Anyone should be able to join a Bible study group, but a leadership training group should be by invitation only. If the group is a major part of the church's pastoral care network then each member needs to be part of a group (at least in theory). But if the group is a special interest group, then it will involve only those who are committed to exploring that particular area of ministry.

What criteria will be used for reviewing the groups?

The criteria for a mission task group will be whether or not the task has been realistically addressed or accomplished. There will be an objectivity to the review. With a kinship group there will be a more subjective element in the review. Has a sense of community and belonging been developing?

How will the groups be supervised?

Will they function as a general group and therefore probably be supervised by the overall pastoral team of the church, or will the group be a special sort of group that requires distinctive supervision? Will the supervision be built in regularly as a matter of course, or will it be a question of group leaders approaching a supervisor when needed? (Which is usually when a problem has grown too big!)

So the first issue is to decide on the specific purpose for which you want to use small groups in your local church setting. Because small groups are so flexible, the chances are that there will be a range of purposes and types of groups happily co-existing at any given time.

A Strategy for Small Groups

Let us imagine that we are beginning with a clean sheet as far as a small group ministry is concerned. How do we go about putting together a strategy for small group ministry development? The following areas would certainly be on my agenda if I was wanting to develop small groups in any future church or ministry, given Roberta Hestenes' definition of small groups:

A Christian small group can be defined as a deliberate face to face gathering of three to twelve people who meet regularly and share the common purpose of exploring together some aspect of the Christian faith and discipleship.

Educate people using appropriate means

It is important that people are given good reasons for the development of small group ministry. Remember that in a church with no history of small groups, this will imply change. Change is facilitated where there is good motivation. This motivation can come about in different ways.

One would be a programme of teaching and preaching to the church on the biblical importance of community and the potential of small groups for the development of this side of the church's life.

Another would be to expose the congregation to models of small group ministry. Some people think conceptually while others do not. To give some people the opportunity to see groups in other situations, or possibly invite a team in from another church to share some of their experiences of small groups, could really help with motivation.

A third approach would be to bring someone in to the local church who is experienced in motivating churches in this area of ministry. There are various consultants around who are willing to spend some of their time doing this.

A fourth approach would be to invite a number of key people who are either 'opinion leaders' in the congregation, or potential small group leaders, to be part of the small group experience over a period of six months or so to give them a taste of the possibilities.

Each of these approaches will deliver the church and its leaders from diving in too soon with an approach to small groups which is not considered or thought through.

Gather a support group who are dynamically interested

By this I do not mean people who will fight for your cause! I am referring to a group, however small, of people who have energy to give to the development of small group ministry within the congregation. Look for those who begin to respond to the previous educational stage. Discover if there are people who have had good experiences of small groups in other situations. Let them operate with you as a sort of think tank.

Ensure good communication with church leadership

Whether it be the deacons, the PCC, the elders, or whatever, they must know what is going on. While some of these people may not be in your support group, it is absolutely vital that they are aware of the development of the vision.

Examine what is already happening

Some churches have small groups in existence without

realising it. In some cases these are 'meetings' of one sort or another which are part of the church's life, but which do not operate with the insights of small groups, and which at times lack purpose. Work with such groups where possible and let a new sense of purpose breathe life into the groups. In other cases there are informal groups operative already: perhaps a small group of parents who meet at the school gate and spend an hour over a cup of coffee with some regularity. Maybe you could talk with such an informal group about the possibility of drawing one or two others in who are not Christians and maybe adding an occasional faith-sharing element. Let us make sure that we are using what is already there, but making sure that we are leaving ownership of the group with the members. Our task is to be a resource for the groups.

Let me give one brief example that has occurred this week. I was invited along to a ministers' fraternal in another part of London to talk about some self-awareness groups I am involved in leading at Spurgeon's College. The ministers were really interested and thought it was good for the students. One of the ministers went on to say that it would be great if they could have such a group, but that there was simply not enough time regularly. I pointed out the obvious. The fraternal spends four hours together on a monthly basis. Some of what they do they are all equally bored with. Why not use the time to engage in some self-awareness work? What they spend on an outside speaker every month could be spent on bringing in a group facilitator. No new commitments are required in terms of additional time etc. But the group could take on a whole new meaning.

Research your potential group members

Given the overall definition and purpose of small groups that we have borrrowed from Roberta Hestenes, there are many types of groups that we can use. It is important that they are the sorts of groups that potential members will be drawn to and motivated for.

Some 'market research' can helpfully be done here and enquiries made of members as to what type of group they would value being a part of.

Small groups work for a variety of reasons. Commonly, some groups gel because they are 'peer' type groups, and others because of a strong sense of shared purpose or task. Some work because of good leadership, and some because of geographical closeness so that the members of the group see one another regularly outside of the group.

Discover whether potential members would warm most to the idea of geographical groupings or task groupings. There could well be room for each type in an average church small group ministry over the course of twelve months.

In addition to discovering from your potential group members their preferences, as already mentioned, you could also find out what major thrust they would want in a small group experience. Roberta Hestenes in her course at Fuller Seminary, 'Building Christian Community Through Small Groups' refers to five basic types of groups:

Study Groups, which can be Bible study, book study, whether Christian or other, pastor's or local church materials.

Sharing and Support Groups, which can be either general

or focused on specific needs (eg, parenting, early marriage, singleness).

Ministry Groups, which can be accountability groups, mission or task groups and committee/community groups.

Covenant Groups, which would include a mixture of Bible study, worship, prayer and ministry to each other.

House Church Groups, which would have a larger membership and would major on worship, teaching and exercise of spiritual gifts.[1]

Or to use John Mallison's categories:

Contact Groups; Interest Groups; Special Groups; Discussion/Study Groups; Therapy Groups; Bible Study Groups; Prayer Groups; Sharing Groups; Personal Growth Groups; Task Groups; Outreach Groups.[2]

Locate and train leaders

The next chapter will major on leadership for small groups, but we mention it here as obviously groups need leaders. This process can take some months to deal with thoroughly.

Publicise groups to the congregation

Make it clear what the options are and what the basic commitments are that will be essential for the different types of groups you might be using. This needs to be done in a variety of ways, but certainly has to include a personal approach to each person who has indicated interest in being part of a small group. This personal approach is probably best done by the leader of the small group that best matches the sort of group which the individual has talked about in the research stage. This seems like a lot of work, but is well worth the effort.

Develop and make available resources for small group leaders

Again we will cover this in the next chapter, but the coordinator of small group ministries needs to be prepared to take this aspect of the work on board. The leaders need servicing.

Establish a positive and regular review system

This needs to be built into the group itself through the contracting process I have referred to earlier (Chapter 2). But also the coordinator of small groups needs to be sure that the group leaders (and members if possible) actually review progress with her or him at regular intervals in a positive exercise, rather than wait for the group to run into heavy water.

Be clear on basic future policies regarding group start-ups or closedowns

Given that part of the contracting process within the group is to do with the duration of the group, it is important to think through an approach to the question of what happens if the group is not working out. Some groups and leaders suffer in silence for much longer than they need to. I believe that a helpful policy is to have regular reviews between the leader and coordinator. If through these reviews it becomes clear that things are not working out, then it is helpful for the coordinator to go in for a session with the group to see if there is something that can helpfully be done to facilitate the group becoming more healthy again. However, if this does not work, then I believe it is important that the group is free to discontinue without any pressure being put on to 'make it work'.

Equally, a policy needs to be thought through with regard to groups that might arise from grass roots within the church: what John Mallison refers to as 'Spontaneous Groups'. I believe that the small group coordinator should be given authority to explore these groups with the individuals concerned to see if there are ways that the church can serve these groups. But basically the policy needs to be positive rather than defensive. Good communication is the key.

6

Developing and Caring for Leaders

As in all other areas of the life of the local church, this is the issue that causes 'the rubber to meet the road'. If small groups are to function helpfully, then there is a need for people who will be prepared to take on the responsibility of leading them; people who are not only willing, but equipped and able to do so.

Really there are three basic issues with regard to a small group ministry in the local church. The first two, the issues of purpose and strategy, we have looked at already. Now we move on to the third, leadership.

Sometimes within the Christian church we have been bad at leadership development and care. No doubt this is because of many of the other pressures of time in local church life. But certainly the Administry organisation's training course title, 'You'll Soon Pick It Up', tends to sum up certain attitudes to leadership development and care.

Variety of Leaders

First, in the sort of cohesive yet mixed approach to small group ministry which has been suggested in this booklet, there is a need for a variety of types of leaders. Roberta Hestenes of Fuller Seminary refers to the following types of leaders if the mixed approach is to flourish:

First there is the need for 'facilitators'. These are the people who lead small groups which have been designed by others, and who use materials provided by others for small group use.

Secondly there is the need for 'creators'. These small group leaders are able to design their own groups or adapt materials and/or create new kinds of groups with different people or to meet new needs.

Thirdly there is the need for coordinators. These are the people who supervise more than one group, and who serve these groups and their leaders with provision of helpful information, facilitation of communication, problem solving skills and general encouragement.

Fourthly there is a need for 'strategists'. These people put together materials and structures for recruiting, developing, training and encouraging other leaders and members.[1]

All that is being suggested is that there are different functions of leadership in the local church as far as small groups are concerned. If this range of functions is being carried out then the chances are that a helpful small group ministry is in operation. Often the fourth category of leader can actually be provided by the input of people from outside of the local situation, providing they understand the dynamics of the local situation.

Alternatively such a person might be available within a group of churches.

Selection and Supervision

Secondly we move on to the selection and supervision of small group leaders. How do you go about choosing people, and, once chosen, how do you go about helping them to do the job as well as it can be done?

There are a number of related matters here including selection, training, supervision and resourcing.

Let us look first of all at *selection*. (Here I am not addressing issues that will be part of some local churches' policy on suitability for leadership – eg, should leaders always be married, should they be male, etc? I personally believe that there are far more important criteria with regard to selection. We would be happy for married, single, female or male leaders to function as small group leaders in our own setting.)

Leaders of small groups need to be primarily people who are growing in their own life in Christ. One of the greatest resources you have to offer in leading a small group is yourself, and your own commitment to growth and development personally. As you are growing as a leader then those around you will be challenged, encouraged, or stimulated to growth.

Then leaders of small groups need to be characterised by attitudes which are secure, positive, and confident. (Or, if you like, 'full of faith'.) Some groups seem to be characterised by inferiority, insecurity and negativity. This is the sort of soil in which little growth takes place. This is not to say that those who are secure and positive will never have problems, or never feel down – we are talking about the basic mood of their life.

A third trait to look for in selection of leaders is that

we should be looking for team people, rather than prima donnas. Within most teams, one person will become a focal point, but always they function as part of a team. Leadership is supremely to reflect the relationships of love and servanthood which Jesus commanded. Prima donnas, solo pilots, or individualists tend to find these relationships and priorities difficult.

Another quality to look for in selection of leaders is evidence of faithfulness in other commitments, such as the individual's involvement in existing small groups, and involvement in the Sunday worship life of the congregation. There is a need for leaders who will model active involvement in basic church commitments so that members of groups do not begin to see their small group as an end in itself.

Other qualities that can be helpful for the small group leader include the ability to initiate and an evidence that this person is a 'people person', as the leadership of a small group will need both of these qualities.

The next major area is that of *training* of small group leaders. Sometimes people join the church who seem to be 'sent from heaven' as far as small group leadership is concerned. Occasionally there will be others who are natural leaders. But most of us need some basic and ongoing training if we are to function to the fullest extent in small group leadership.

Training can take various forms. The important lesson to learn is that listening to someone speaking about how to lead small groups is not sufficient for a total approach to small groups leadership training.

One approach to leadership training favoured by some is what could be referred to as a 'Model Group'. In this two trained leaders, who also have skills in training others, give a model small group experience to trainees over a period of months. First the trainers model the skills of small group leadership so that the trainees begin to get the feel of a good group experience and also have the opportunity to reflect on and discuss the contributory factors and skills. Then the trainees take turns in leading different aspects of the group, with helpful feedback from other group members. If the resources and the time are available, this seems one of the best approaches to training. Often, however, in the local church the need for new leaders is more urgent!

Other approaches include short courses of four to eight weeks' duration in which skills are explored. Intensive workshop weekends can pack a lot into a short time. Then there is the approach, probably best married to the short course approach, which majors on weekly supervision groups for a period of time, such as three months, in which newly trained and commissioned leaders meet together with a supervisor to talk back on their experience in the small group setting. Another approach which requires a lot of time is one-to-one training and supervision with one trainer sitting in with a trainee and teaching in that context.

The tools to be used in the training are basically threefold. There is a theoretical dimension which is relevant to the course approach and the on-the-job approach. The other two tools are the on-the-job method or the training course approach. If the on-the-job method is used, the learning material and experience can be the group itself. If the course approach is used, some helpful training methods include role play, discussion, case studies, skills training, production of sample group programmes and more formal input.

As to the content of such training, this will largely depend on the style and emphasis of the local church. Some will want to major heavily on communication skills, others on approaches to Bible study, and yet others on spiritual gifts and mutual ministry. However, the principles of training outlined above will serve various areas of training need.

Now we move on to *supervision* of those who are involved in small group leadership.

Sometimes, even when training is provided and a lot of initial encouragement is offered to new leaders, we can still fall down in this area of supervision. A church operating with small groups certainly needs to make provision for realistic supervision. This means provision of a context in which small group leaders can share with someone whose role is to be supportive. The small group leader can share how the group is developing; any difficulties that the group or the leader is encountering; and how the task of leadership is affecting the small group leader. At times such sessions will be tales of encouragement, and at other times concerns will be shared, but always the leader will feel supported and not alone.

Within our own church we have operated with two different systems of supervision at different times. First group supervision when ten to twelve small group leaders meet with two supervisors for a couple of hours to talk about how things are going. They share problems for corporate wisdom, do some training, and provide a context of prayer and worship in which the leaders of the small groups can be ministered to and offer ministry while not being the responsible person.

A second model we have used is personal supervision. At times this has operated with some of our elders being available to individual leaders. At other times I have fulfilled this role and given each small group leader two hours on three occasions each year. During these times they can share whatever they want. In addition the small group leaders can always come with any emergencies they might have.

The important thing is that such leaders feel part of a team. This inevitably encourages loyalty on the part of the small groups towards the local church as well as serving the small group leader.

The fourth area under selection and supervision of leaders is that of *resourcing*. There are all sorts of materials available these days for small groups to make use of (see appendix). The task of those who oversee the small group ministry is to be regularly offering materials and putting together a resource centre which is available to small group leaders. This will include Bible study materials, tapes, videos, group games and exercises, other study materials, etc. It is unrealistic to imagine that the typical small group leader will have the time to research all that is available in terms of materials, so this is a way in which the church can serve its small group leaders.

One final matter under this area of caring for leaders through selection and supervision is the provision of what some would call a *job description*. It is important that when a potential small group leader is being approached, that future leader is given clear outlines of what is expected, what support will be offered, how long the appointment is likely to be for, and what degree of freedom and initiative can be exercised.

A sample is provided by Anton Baumohl in *Grow Your Own Leaders*:[2]

Job Description for a House Group Leader

Job Title: House Group Leader
Responsible To: Member of pastoral team/elder/minister.
Responsible For: All members of the house group.

Working Relationship With: The minister/elders/members of pastoral team/other house group leaders/house group members.

Nature and Purpose of Job: The role is primarily to enable the group to function effectively. One person will not possess all the gifts necessary to ensure the successful life of a house group. The house group leader needs to be sensitive to the whole group and to the needs of the individuals in that group. The leader will then work with God and the group members to ensure that those needs are met. House group leaders make an initial commitment of two years to this work, after which their responsibilities are reviewed.

Major Tasks: 1 To arrange the regular fortnightly meetings and to ensure that there is appropriate hospitality.

2 To help create an accepting and caring atmosphere that encourages members to develop deeper relationships.

3 To act as a link between the leadership of the church and the members of the house group.

4 To help people discover their role as Christians in the church and in the wider community.

5 To encourage everyone to have an active involvement in the group. The leader has the ultimate responsibility for the pastoral care of the group even though he or she may share this task with others in the group.

6 To ensure that any group study programme

is well prepared, adapted to suit the group
and properly led.

7 To ensure their own continuing development as leaders by attending monthly meetings and training courses as and when
arranged.

Skills Needed

Thirdly we move on to the skills with which small group
leaders need to be equipped. (We need to underline
here that we are dealing with group skills and not basic
personal character and spirituality. These need to be
evidenced in the initial selection stage as outlined earlier
in this chapter.)

First small group leaders need some awareness of
small group processes.

The experience of being together with others in a
small group which is making living contact together is
the experience of a journey or pilgrimage. As on any
journey, even an often-repeated one, there will be distinctive experiences for each group. But there will also
be certain common landmarks and transitions that the
group passes through on its pilgrimage together. To
begin to understand something of these common landmarks of development will enable the small group
leader to help the group to understand what it is
experiencing together, and thus be better able to lead
the group.

It is important to understand, for example, that each
group you are leading has three major needs (as shown
in the interlocking circles below). Each has implications
for the others. The small group leader and the group
need to develop strategies for helping the group with its
task needs, maintenance needs and individual needs.

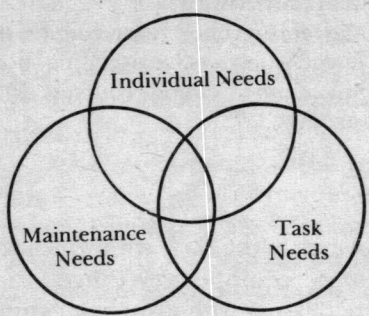

Individual Needs

Maintenance Needs

Task Needs

The task need is the need for the group to achieve the common task. (Hence again the need for good initial contracting so that each member is clear on the agreed major task or purpose.)

The maintenance need is the need for the group to hold itself together and for the members to maintain themselves as cohesive units.

The individual need is for the group to make provision for meeting the needs of the individuals which are inevitably brought into the group.

John Adair in *Effective Leadership* makes the following comments which will help a small group leader to see the significance of each of these circles of need.

But first cover the task circle with a disc. See what it does to the maintenance and the individual circles. So, 'If a group fails in its task, this will intensify the disintegrative tendencies present in the *group* and diminish the satisfaction of *individual* needs.'[3]

Now cover the maintenance circle with a disc. See what it does to the task and individual circles. So, 'If there is a lack of unity or harmonious relationships in the group, this will affect performance of the *task* or *individual* needs.'⁴

Now cover the individual circle with a disc. See what happens to the task and the maintenance circles. So, 'If an individual feels frustrated and unhappy, he will not make his maximum contribution to either the common *task* or to the *life* of the group.'⁵

Then also to be aware of some of the stages that a group goes through in its lifecycle is very helpful for the small group leader. There are various models, but I find the following the most helpful.

In the first stage of *exploration* we each evaluate whether or not we feel a part of the group, particularly in the areas of people, purpose and power. Hence the importance again of the contracting process, and also the freedom of individuals as far as possible to choose to which group they will belong. This is the time when we discover if we share ownership of the group or whether the group is owned (or controlled) by the leader. Questions such as, 'Am I listened to?', 'Do I feel as if I belong with these people?' and 'Do I want to spend my time doing these activities?' are asked, either consciously or not.

Here the leader's task is to work at including people and guaranteeing everyone a hearing. Also protection of those members who might be feeling vulnerable. The leader provides security and order.

In the second stage of *transition* we move into the post-honeymoon phase. We come face to face with who we really are in the group. The leader's task in this stage is to facilitate good communication and help the group to work through its needs. How this is handled will govern whether the group grows through this stage, or settles either for unreality or breakup.

In the third stage of *action*, having worked through various issues with honesty and grace, the group members will grow in freedom to act and initiate. There will be a strong sense of 'this is our group'. Members will know that risk taking is okay. During this stage the group will accomplish a lot. The leader encourages the group in its initiatives while at the same time keeping the group on course for its agreed purpose and destination.

In the fourth stage of *termination* the group will celebrate the good times together and affirm one another in various ways. They will reflect on what they have learned and how they have grown. They will work through their feelings as they move towards a new group. In this stage, the leader's task is to model the sort of openness and vulnerability required if this process is to be worked through, and also to model positive attitudes towards the new thing which lies ahead. Small groups are always only for a season.

These skills with regard to group processes are basic for any training of small group leaders. But in addition there will be skills needed which will be appropriate to the types of groups operating and the emphasis of the church. Certainly I believe that necessary skills include delegation, Bible study approaches, and communication skills – how to listen, how to ask questions and how to share yourself.

Functions of a leader

Fourthly, and finally, we move on to some of the functions of the small group leader. Eddie Gibbs in his *I Believe in Church Growth* describes the perfect small group leader (but realise that no such perfect leader exists, which is why all group leaders and members need the love which the New Testament speaks of):

Someone who can develop inter-personal relationships.

76

Therefore she/he needs to be a secure person; relaxed and restrained; calm and objective; ... displaying a loving concern for each person in the group with an understanding and generous attitude which covers the faults of others. Sensitive to atmosphere and able to display tact and apply anti-freeze to thaw out tense situations. Enthusiastic about the group, she/he is teachable and does not need to pretend to know all the right answers ... and is always appreciative of the comments of others.[6]

So the first function of the leader is to model the style of relationships (open and truthful) and exhibit the sort of attitudes (loving and servant-like) which will help the group to relate in ways which are conducive to the deepening of relationships and sharing together. Modelling is vital. In small groups we primarily lead by example as our lives touch each other.

The second function of a leader is to enable the group firstly to agree its objectives and purposes, and then, secondly, to facilitate it in achieving those objectives. The leader is not the expert or the teacher, but rather the enabler and facilitator of the other members of the group in their purpose. Small group leaders who are experts tend to kill groups stone dead!

The third function of a small group leader will be to make sure that the group, its members and its activities are well prayed for. This will help the leader and the group to realise whom the group is ultimately for, and also the resources which are available for the group in its pursuit of Christian growth.

The fourth function is to ensure that adequate preparation has been carried out prior to each meeting. This involves mundane but essential things like letting people know when and where the meeting will occur; seeing that hospitality is available (a room not too cold, too hot, or too noisy); guaranteeing that any resources needed for the evening are available and that personnel-wise, people know if they have particular responsibilities prior to the meeting.

The fifth function is that of caring. Not that the leader will do all of this, but that the leader will model caring and encourage others in it. The leader will certainly care for individuals by supporting those who seem to be under seige within the group, ignored by the group or left alone with their hurts.

It goes without saying therefore, that the leader needs to learn to delegate – otherwise you'll have lots of burnt out small group leaders on your hands!

Conclusion

How it Works Out in One Local Church

Some years ago I was on a week's course at Surrey University. The course was on counselling and was being run by a Christian agency. As the week progressed I became increasingly frustrated with the approach used by the course leaders. They made everything seem so simple and straightforward with four principles for this and five steps to that. Having been involved in counselling, I knew it was not that simple.

The most helpful session was the final one when the associate leader stood at the overhead projector and began to talk. He spoke of how straightforward all these principles seemed. As he continued to talk, he began to do a doodle on a sheet of acetate. The doodle went all over the sheet, meandering, at times turning back on itself. He ended up by saying that although he believed the principles were true, nevertheless in practice the journey can often be anything but clear ... a little like the doodle.

There is a huge danger in a booklet like this of sharing certain insights and principles and giving the impression that if you follow them, everything will be straightforward. In this conclusion I would like to correct that impression in case anyone has picked it up. I want to do this by giving a brief outline of small group ministry in the church I know best, here in Streatham.

The story of the past seven years in our own small group ministry has been one of ebb and flow, developing in our understanding of some of the principles outlined here, at times putting them into practice, and at other times forgetting or compromising. We have had some very meaningful groups and others which are unlikely to live on in anyone's memory. There have been times when our small groups have been rich in life and other times when they have been somewhat stagnant and have needed change and renewal.

The Lord has regularly had to renew us with the sort of vision outlined in the introduction to this booklet. We are often short of leaders, not because we don't apply the training principles, but because we are in an area where many people move in and then move out to suburbia. Often other churches will be getting the benefit of the training we have given. In our gracious moments this is fine, but at other times, when we are pushed for a leader or two, the dominant feeling is not one of grace but of frustration!

We have had seasons without small groups, but always we come back to them as a structure which can serve the development of Christians in all sorts of ways.

And we have seen people changed. Some have been

cared for and encouraged. Some have begun to minister for the first time, and others have prayed aloud for the first time. Some have shared their hopes and fears with another person for the first time in a long time, while others have sadly turned away as they could not cope with the pain and challenge of growth and truthfulness at such close quarters.

We have learned that with small group ministry you can never be so foolish as to imagine that you have found the answer and that they can be left to run themselves for the next five years – or even for the next five months – but they can be a resource well worth the effort and care taken over them.

We have seen their benefits in Bible study groups, growth groups, training groups, prayer groups, support groups, outreach groups and task groups of various shapes and sizes. My hope is that this will become an increasingly significant ministry among us. It will, providing that in our pursuit of small group ministry, our vision of what could be does not become more important than the people who make them up. Bonhoeffer in his *Life Together* says, 'He who loves his dream of community more than the Christian community itself, becomes a destroyer of the latter, even though his personal intentions may be ever so honest and earnest and sacrificial.'[1]

Equally, our vision of small groups can be the destroyer of fellowship and growth, unless it is blended with a real love for those with whom we are relating.

Nermal could not have been very satisfied with Garfield's answers. I hope that our answers in this booklet have been a lot more helpful and realistic.

APPENDIX

Resources for Small Groups

Group Games, Exercises, Relationship Building:

Grigor, Jean. *Grow to Love*. St Andrew Press: Edinburgh, 1977.

Nelson-Jones, Richard. *Human Relationship Skills*. Cassell: Eastbourne, 1986.

Mallison, John. *Creative Ideas for Small Groups*. Scripture Union: London, 1978.

Remocker, A Jane and Storch, Elizabeth T. *Actions Speak Louder*. Churchill Livingstone: Edinburgh, 1977.

Approaches to Bible Study:

Materials from –

Scripture Union
Navigators
Bible Society
CPAS
Serendipity
Victor Elective Study Books and Guides.

Bibliography

Adair, John. *Effective Leadership*. Pan Books: London, 1983.

Anderson, Ray and Guernsey, Dennis B. *On Being Family*. Eerdmans: Grand Rapids, 1985.

Augsburger, David. *Caring Enough To Confront*. Marshalls: Basingstoke, 1985.

Banks, Robert. *All The Business Of Life*. Albatross Books: NSW, 1987.

Banks, Julia and Robert. *The House Church*. Albatross Books: NSW, 1986.

Baumohl, Anton. *Grow Your Own Leaders*. Scripture Union: London, 1987.

Baumohl, Anton. *Making Adult Disciples*. Scripture Union: London, 1984.

Bolt, Martin and Myers, David. *The Human Connection*. Hodder & Stoughton: London, 1985.

Bonhoeffer, Dietrich. *Life Together*. SCM: London, 1954.

Cotterell, Peter. *All About House Groups*. Kingsway: Eastbourne, 1985.

Douglas, Tom. *Basic Groupwork*. Tavistock Publications: London, 1978.

Driver, John. *Community and Commitment*. Herald Press: Scottdale, 1976.

Edge, Findley. *The Greening Of The Church*. Word Books: Waco, 1971.

Gibbs, Eddie. *I Believe In Church Growth*. Hodder & Stoughton: London, 1981.

Girard, Robert. *Brethren Hang Together*. Zondervan: Grand Rapids, 1979.

Gish, Art. *Living In Christian Community*. Albatross Books: NSW, 1979.

Grigor, Jean. *Grow To Love*. St Andrew Press: Edinburgh, 1977.

Hestenes, Roberta. *Using the Bible In Groups*. The Westminster Press: Philadelphia, 1983.

Hestenes, Roberta. *Building Christian Community Through Small Groups*. Fuller Theological Seminary: Pasadena Ca, 1985.

Hill, Brian. *The Greening of Christian Education*. Lancer Books: NSW, 1985.

Hoekema, Anthony. *Created in God's Image*. Eerdmans: Grand Rapids, 1986.

Jones, Gordon. *Design For Learning*. Falcon Press: London, 1974.

Mallison, John. *Building Small Groups In The Christian Community*. Scripture Union: London, 1978.

Mallison, John. *Creative Ideas For Small Groups In The Christian Community*. Scripture Union: London, 1978.

Osmaston, Amiel. *Sharing The Life*. Grove Books: Nottingham, 1979.

Peace, Richard. *Small Group Evangelism.* Scripture Union: London, 1987.

Prior, David. *The Church In The Home.* Marshalls: Basingstoke, 1983.

Richards, Lawrence. *A New Face For The Church.* Zondervan: Grand Rapids, 1970.

Richards, Lawrence. *69 Ways To Start A Study Group And Keep It Going.* Zondervan: Grand Rapids, 1973.

Richards, Lawrence and Hoeldtke, Clyde. *A Theology of Church Leadership.* Zondervan: Grand Rapids, 1980.

Snyder, Howard. *New Wineskins.* Marshall, Morgan and Scott: London, 1975.

Snyder, Howard. *The Radical Wesley.* IVCF: Illinois, 1980.

Tillapaugh, Frank. *Unleashing the Church.* Regal Books: Ventura Ca, 1982.

Williams, Michael. *Learning Through Experience.* Grove Books: Nottingham, 1981.

Notes

Introduction

1 J R W Stott, *Issues Facing Christians Today* (Marshalls: 1984), p 328.

Chapter 1

1 A A Hoekema, *Created in God's Image* (Eerdmans/Paternoster: 1986), p 76.
2 *ibid*, p 77.
3 D Bonhoeffer, *Life Together* (SCM Press Ltd: 1954), pp 86–87.
4 L Coleman, *Serendipity Leaders' Guide* (Scripture Union: 1985), p 16.

Chapter 2

1 *op cit*, pp 78–79.
2 R S Anderson and D B Guernsey, *On Being Family* (Eerdmans: 1985), p 80.

Chapter 3

1 R C Girard, *Brethren Hang Together* (Zondervan Corp: 1979), back cover.
2 J Driver, *Community and Commitment* (Herald Press: 1976), p 28.
3 A Gish, *Living in Christian Community* (Herald Press: 1979), p 18.
4 R Hestenes, *Using The Bible In Groups* (Westminster Press: 1983), p 21.
5 H Snyder, *New Wineskins* (Marshalls: 1977), p 130.
6 L Richards and C Hoeldtke, *A Theology of Church Leadership* (Zondervan: 1980), p 309.

Chapter 4

1 This model is explored by Peter Wagner in *Your Church Can Grow* (Regal Books: 1976).

Chapter 5

1 *op cit*.
2 J Mallison, *Building Small Groups and The Christian Community* (Scripture Union: 1978).

Chapter 6

1 R Hestenes, *Building Christian Community Through Small Groups* (Fuller Seminary: 1985), p 96.
2 A Baumohl, *Grow Your Own Leaders* (Scripture Union: 1987), pp 61–62.
3 J Adair, *Effective Leadership* (Pan: 1983), p 38.
4 *ibid*, p 39.
5 *ibid*, p 39.
6 E Gibbs, *I Believe In Church Growth* (Hodder & Stoughton: 1981), p 261.

Conclusion

1 *op cit*, pp 15–16.

Keith Roberts, together with some colleagues, runs a consultancy and training ministry to different churches and groups in the area of small group ministry. If you would like to contact him to talk over any of the issues raised here or for any other matter relating to small groups, including training events, then please write to him at:

'Encounter'
Mitcham Lane Baptist Church
230 Mitcham Lane
STREATHAM
London SW16 6NT

The Authority Of Scripture

by Andrew Rigden Green

'When asked to defend the authority of the Bible, Charles Spurgeon retorted, "You don't need to defend a lion, just let it out of its cage."'

Today we live in a sceptical age where truth seems uncertain and authority is questioned.

How can we defend the claim, so crucial to evangelical belief, that Scripture is the word of God, and as such our supreme authority?

With refreshing clarity and sharp observation, Andrew Rigden Green marshals together the most salient points in the debate about The Book:

- the authority of Scripture and the authority of God
- revelation—the liberal, neo-orthodox and evangelical positions
- inspiration and accuracy
- interpretation—non-evangelical and evangelical approaches
- implications of authority—living under the word.

ANDREW RIGDEN GREEN is Senior Pastor of Upton Vale Baptist Church, Torquay.

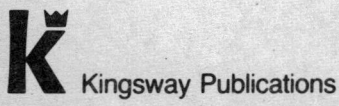

Kingsway Publications

Pastors Under Pressure

by Paul Beasley-Murray

Why are pastors burning out?

A frighteningly large number of pastors today are leaving their posts because of the strain. Many more hang on grimly, battered by pressures they often barely understand. Expectations of pastors remain immense and unrealistic.

Paul Beasley-Murray, who spent thirteen years in pastoral ministry before becoming Principal of Spurgeon's College, has made a careful study of the stresses on church leaders. His succinct analysis and pointed recommendations make a lot of sense. *Pastors Under Pressure* will prove essential reading not only for pastors but for their congregations: 'the task is made bearable when the ministry of believers is taken seriously.'

THE REV DR PAUL BEASLEY-MURRAY is series editor of Spurgeon's Booklets, of which this is the first volume. The concise and inexpensive Booklets will cover a wide variety of pastoral issues.

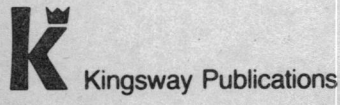

Kingsway Publications

The Activist's Guide to Prayer

by Bryan Gilbert

Christian activists find it hard to have a meaningful prayer life. The author, a self-confessed activist, has drawn upon his own experience and wide reading to help those who want to deepen their relationship with God.

So often the 'door' has been shut from our side, frequently by our own Christian busyness. In a series of short pertinent chapters Bryan Gilbert shows how we can not only turn the key and open the door, but step through it. Without prayer, we shall be powerless. With prayer, we shall be strong.

THE REV BRYAN GILBERT, a Baptist minister, has been International Director of One Step Forward Ministries and Evengelism Training Consultant for The Bible Society, and more recently Field Director for Mission 89. He is author of *Fruit of the Spirit* (also published by Kingsway). He lives in Swindon.

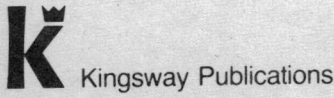

Kingsway Publications